The Dropping of Petals

The Dropping of Petals

Eliza O'Toole

MUSCALIET

Published by Muscaliet
Chelmsford, Essex, United Kingdom
www.muscaliet.co.uk

First published 2021 in paperback
Design and typesetting by Simon Everett
Typeset in Bembo and Europa
Printed by Imprint Digital, Devon

All rights reserved

Text, artwork and images © Eliza O'Toole, 2021

The rights of Eliza O'Toole to be identified as the author of this work have been asserted in accordance with Copyright, Design and Patents Act 1988

Cover artwork adapted from 'Daffodils' by Eliza O'Toole, pen and ink, printed in full pp.38–39

Other images: 'Stones', pen and ink, shown opposite; 'Ink Caps', pen and ink, p.71, both by Eliza O'Toole

ISBN 978-1-912616-14-5

1 2 3 4 5 6 7 8 9 10
First Edition

reworking the
ground

stones flung loose

Acknowledgements

Holly Pester, Philip Terry, James Canton, Chris McCully all walked with me here, and I salute the width of their horizons and generosity. To Muscaliet, for roundly ignoring Don Marquis's aphorism, 'Publishing a volume of verse is like dropping a rose petal down the Grand Canyon and waiting for the echo' and for recognising a kindred kind, and first and foremost to my editors Simon Everett and Moyra Tourlamain for their insightful assistance and unstinting belief in the multivalency of my work, my appreciation is boundless.

To Martin, Emily, Joe and, as the crow flies 10, 810 miles from here, to Tom

Contents

Land law	5
Shimmers between	7
Pollarded oak, East Anglian Sanatorium	11
Stour Owls January 28th	12
Lemon Wong, Leadenham Low Fields	13
Cover Seeds	14
How to Grow Mistle Toe	16
Under standing trees	18
At the edge of April	21
Field Incapacity	22
Tree Climbers	25
Falling in Autumn	26
Take a leaf	29
Being with trees	30
The breaking of Spring	31
The bending of Summer	32
Poet's tree	35
Inside February	36
Oak and Owl	37
Obstructing a carriageway	40
January 7th	43
Gold dust	44
Belonging	47
Walking a way	48
A shovel of land	49
Clarson v. Arnold (1890), 54 J.P. 630	50
Between materiality and semiosis, or Suppose a rose	53
In the margins with March	56

Apoptosis	58
Garden walls	59
Dead mole in fresh owl pellet	60
Growing things	61
Petals	62
Composition	63
Tines catch a rabbit	64
Home grown	65
Wild the why	66
Familial Tree	67
Sky, hardened	68
Notes	70

The Dropping of Petals

Land law

Little lanes rutted with rivulets of rain, leaf litter and layers of traces of Charolais, hollow ways over arched with blasted haw and small leaved limes, soaked oaks, birches, and spilling celandine.

In other words

Language as law is a different species to language as meaning, meaning-making, referent or identifier. Stranglehold.

Furrowed fields in February, porous space of elastic energy; of contraction and expansion, of passage, of potency: threshold, sentient, sense-maker and shaper, concealing and revealing, liminal and latent, potent with porosity, grown out of the exchange and always already growing again, accumulating humus, bones, stones, little pips of grit, fur, fury and feathered worlds of weatherings.

In other worlds

Land law is a language of land as a conception and as a praxis of governing. Freehold.

In March, monumental, tilled and tilthed, Spring seeded an accumulation threaded through all dimensionally with a dense intensity of epoch and ecology, a transmissive thoroughfare of perpetual exchange and interchange in the lay of the land.

In other words

Interacting with land, the language of law creates a context which contours land differently. Law dissolves land as surely as acid rain. In the wake of that is a shadow, a shadow land, a concept of land, an idea. Ownership.

After rain, aromatic land tastes of grit and sand.

In other worlds

the privileging of conceptual legal language of land (having the physical force of law) over the materiality of language that is the lore of the land renders land asunder, immaterial, stones flung loose. W/rent.

The suspicion of a wall, the sun shards and a pot falls soil scatters how stones and things break speculate earth shards found pulled out stones a toad and tangled roots net palimpsest, the soil changes and it rains.

Shimmers between

Lodged seedlike
in the clay of it, amidst a petrichor as particular as this summer rain
through claggy cretaceous chalk glacially grounded
together the land and I, prepositional, gathered
with flint and poplars valleying fluvial till, flanking small leaved
limes, stand.

The land flows seamlessly here sheared with chalk, clay lands under cleaving
streams jumbling little stones over and over sand and under deep damp mossed
and brambled under story. This land is cleft and heaved
with all the traceability of etymology, mired in the word of it,
manifest
materially as missing, and in its roots anchored and as long as lost
thread webbed in vertical archaeology and sky-notated snagging clouds
and through brachial tracery, that star shot.

Unmoored, they are,
lots of little stones tumbling in the spring fed streams following
the valley left by the Stour through old willow pollards and working wood.
Out with mapped meaning, what are these words saying when they make land fall
as little lines and swirls, as mumbling as grinding as chattering stones
as inert as closed books or seeds sealed in tiny tin foil packets
waiting latent and pluripotent, or desiccated
just like bad lines alienating land on a plan can destroy a world and some,
and all against tradition, always already bound.

This land is what I have
in my hand, lore full, sticky and today heavy and rimed
with frost, lost loess flint filled solid ground aromatic
the tang of winter and wild sage just before the snow comes, and wet

I found

copse shaded
this mud macrocosm of culture and culturing thickening
not a metaphoric mud; this I can smell
loamy land, this I can feel
the grit of it; this horizon rising mist mellowed mired
in the lea of the hill of this shoulder of land.

I find

in rubber boots, knotted hair filled
with burrs, little bones, birds and gritty soil. It is pockets, cuffs and overalls
turn ups mulch-full, sheet weavers and spent mushroom compost. It is the scent of green,
the smell of brown, the stain of loam and sphagnum moss
an echo that preceding thought, before the law, before I am,
a second a nature as that, and in that lore of this symbiotic land,
I found homo and humus intertwined.

In this morning's bruise lilac mist bowls around the oaks
damply and I pick the last of last autumn's leaves from my hair, shivering
slightly as foliose lichens, rhizines inhabiting the old bird cherry boughs
down touching the grass, drip must silver greenly. There is much moss,
lime and springy, haloed in droplets
and through swards of yellow narcissus piss sour and rain bent
the jackdaws are raucous highly polished bitumen black,
vertiginous and now low in vast clattering.
The hens are huddled

I found

under the pollard oak in bark spliced and piled horizontal trunks split shattered sharded
awning branches with slender silver birches peeling among young stands of hazel, catkin
strung lime and latent and cascading all around us, leaf litter a foot deep,

we adrift with feathers and scatters of fur, see bluebells greening

the lemon morning sliding from the surface of the pond,
the sky rising slate grey slanting slow, the puppy shaking and a crowd
collecting in the oak, we are soaked, there are feathers floating
and in last autumns corrugating leaves, spores land. Spring rains.

There is an arresting ambiguity under the oaks, drift snow melting
to humus and hollow warrens. Cow parsley sprung liminal and lacy,
the hens scratch damp earth for worms red threads clawed and clung
and through this slick somatic morning, wet moss and low mist, the ground
rising from the horizon is always already and sliding away

I find

here care sentient and sentinel in the sense of being there,
in shimmers in between,
in mutual standing stood with the oak and paper bark birches
peeling slowly silver slivers uncurling in the rain soaked,
at the conjunction of the word and world, a present in presence.

And in the autumn, I found those innumerable forms, that evolving
evolution of green, that ocean of deprived autotrophic bacteria
and phototrophic metastability. That which, on this autumn evening
heaving heavy with brown, with gold, with bees susurrating softly
feeding in deep purple, with dandelion floss flying and pollen
dusting quake grass seeds, and in gigantic Stipa fronds goldcrests swaying,
and in the tallest of burdock teasels flocking finches, just are.

As now the oaks' lintels and latticework are blackening and propping up
the darkening sky bleeding blood harvest orange to pigeon pink and grey,
and three miles below in bedrock, minerals percolate and in taking them up
this thoracic tree slightly weaves

I found

on days like these
where summer leaves, and leaves burn red and copper curled
that in that matter that is the land that is the law that it transcends
beneath the oak, beneath that tree
it leaves its leaves unhung; flurried from sloughing sky
shed marcescent to lie, dead lettering the ground.

Pollarded oak, East Anglian Sanatorium

stele and cortex
breathing

tensile
strength

tree
roots
strain

the modulus
of elasticity

$T(r)$ $\varepsilon(r)$ $E(r)$

morphological
architecture

anchors

taking rain

Stour Owls January 28th

The dark comes up from the land to meet the call of the tawny owl and the tang of crushed wild sage. Damp soil and holm oaks surround. She calls in the gloaming, ahead and to the left in the brachial tracery of the chestnut. There's no movement, not a breath, no wind. Her calls increase in frequency and in pitch. And to the right, a slight pin thin hoot. He's located her, and then there's deep grey silence, so deep I hear the sky sigh. And then the low slow of a barn owl, as the white slide of her glide brushes the air that we breathe.

[l]i|t|t|Le Lanes

frothy & sheep

woven

Cover seeds

make several holes keep
seeds covered
in the daytime uncover the night
take off when the seeds are half-germinated
plant and be in a state of dormancy in summer and the leaves turn
yellow
beginners should better use sand
cultivate the seeds seeds grow slow in the sand the plants
will be vigorous in the future if you (a) tend
use the other kind of soil, try to use the kind kindred kindling curdled
kind
clay would not be a good choice
should soil be disinfected by microwave oven before it has been used
petrichor will fail then snails
do not break biome make
fallow muck mallow
Pay attention: the surface cloud must not be too dry, which is very
important
when watering, all the sky should be wetted and there is no need to
water a cloudy day
burn after watering, there is no need on a sunny day
it should be supposed
know after weeding
water after bleeding, do not suppress the soil
horizon
bleed after weeding, suppress perilous flutter
byes fly wild oats flip flowers fast
growing grasses
cut after bleeding, reap after weeping
rye
pheasant's eye

late autumn sowing should be avoided
summer sowing should be avoided
avoid sowing before May
sowing should be avoided on Saturn day
and avoid a void and
water
logging on Wednesday
establishment now is appropriate.

How to Grow Mistle Toe

First
The
Seed

Expands

And then

a green hypocotyl
tips towards
the host

with which
it
connects

then
a swelling
haustorium

which
is both host
and
mistle toe

from which
sprouts a sprout
which sprouts a sprout
which sprouts a sprout

which bifurcates

if
you
get the time
right

and
the light
right

and right there
there's
an apple
and a poplar
or
a lime, or an acacia or a hawthorn

tree

and each sprout bifurcates, and each
sprout bifurcates and
each
sprout spouts sprouts and then bifurcates

finally it will bifurcate the

tree.

Under standing trees

In the rain
a gather of earth
and I under the sky

Sycamores syllable saplings
willow words between
the drip and the stop

Crows in rows
on the wire
the jackdaws punctuate

whilst we soak
under a standing
of big old pollard oaks

In the rain
a gather of earth
and I under the sky

Sycamores syllable saplings
willow words between
the drip and the stop

Crows in rows
on the wire
the jackdaws punctuate

whilst we soak
under a standing
of big old pollard oaks

At the Edge of April

It was the sea; it was Prussian blue and grew apple green swept wild in the April wind raked flat and back prone and velvet sheening in the wet light; it was the storey under the oaks soaked pitched and toned out in the sky scratching & the sun rose milkily and low swells nippled in the sea bluely and then purpling bruised sour lemon in the zinc wind swelling as the oaks stroked our faces as we walked. Past. Rinsed, and counting frogspawn into sheltered cold black pools well-watered and the old sun catches ebony and bedazzled bones of soaked oak shaft with silver slivered light damp fern fronds still tight, the smell of ozone salt green garlic tang of ash and blue bells curling.

Field Incapacity

Ownership of the Way

...tute in the highway authority, the herbage (*m*) and the trees ...control (*n*).

...soil.—The owner is entitled to the subsoil absolu... ...t use the soil, or de... ...ith it by breaki... ...t open, or i... ...to interfere w... ...use of it by t... ...ulic for the... (*o*). If he o... ...on both sid... ...he highway... ...el through... ...nder the r... ...ovided he d... ...ably wit... ...t of passa... ...the roa... ab... ...ing right... ...n (*p*). Ap... ...tatut... ...of the sub... ...refor... ...absoil of a h... ...nde... streets... ...Acts, ...e th... ...rial... ...rso... ...se... ...tion

...re Acts frequ... ...y co... ...ain pro... ...ads. In *Neaverson v. Peterborough Ru...l*... ...f a private road was, by an inclosure awa...d made... ...ys to be let for...

A weave
of
trees
                    root
& meet

bed rock

pressure
fissures
as
seeds
feed
& stones grow

sub soil
texture
holds

water
&
worms
&

worms

eventually   leave

                A   weave
                    of
                        trees
root
                & meet

                                            bed rock

        pressure

                        fissures
    as
    seeds
    feed

        & stones grow

      sub   soil
      texture
      holds

            water
              &
            worms
              &
                                        worms

    eventually   leave

Tree Climbers

the
parliament
reconvenes raucously   and rises   as one

the walnut
claws
the
ground

weighted
with
heavy scent

and roses

roses

rising

climb

to
meet

the
black, black,   crows

Falling in Autumn

Dendritic tapestry
Un leafed
crashed canopy

Floored
Split
Like
Infinitives

flawed

A

Sentence
Scattered &
Prostrate

re viewed horizontally
root reaching raw

floored

breaking much
more than law

in a sown seed, a tension and a coherence between form and flowering,
in the wind, lore and phonemes coalescence, and sentences fall
in a word, things break off

that said, the shape of winter is in the hedge,
one morning a flower bursts into flower, a reformation
of bee smoke and dog fox scent in parenthesis, rosemary and rhyme

crows over it, the tree
and everything suspended and stilled in the blanks

in a sown seed, a tension and a coherence between form and flowering,
in the wind, lore and phonemes coalescence, and sentences fall
in a word, things break off

that said, the shape of winter is in the hedge,
one morning a flower bursts into flower, a reformation
of bee smoke and dog fox scent in parenthesis, rosemary and thyme

crows over it, the tree
and everything suspended and stilled in the blanks

Take a leaf

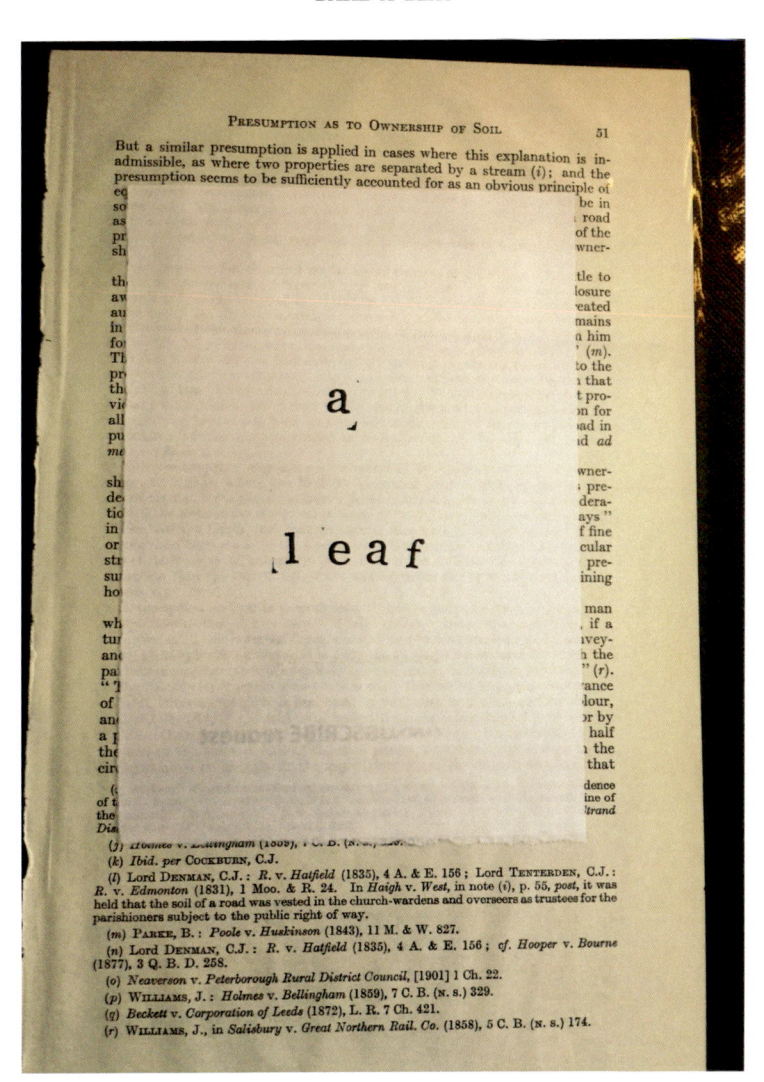

a

leaf

Being with trees

To ross a tree, debark it,
set a drawknife on the branch bark and cut.

To peel a tree, position a knife on the branch bark, and pull downwards
peel the first layer, go for the next line of bark and continue. Use both hands.
Dig deep. Cause injury. Draw the knife towards you.

Leave the tree.
Come back eight months later.

Eight months

For four hundred years this oak, when the rain came, made this land.

Fallen rain percolates and meets fibrous roots feeding close to the surface
minuscule spaces between particles of land fill
and flow upwards to the sky scratching tracery, to the pinnacle.
Root hairs synchronise with soil pores and with darkling beetles and earth,
worms cast crumbs and phosphorous
making middens, making land.

The beech foot spreads   and   spreads
grey lichen lime moss around the bole
where seeds safe harboured in the depression await
light to materialise
and translate sugars into another whiskered ash.

And all along the drip line, leaves pile
whilst under a scant sky, outriggers heavy
touch the treemade ground, earth up
and crystallising time,

they hold up the sky.

The breaking of Spring

This morning
buried radicles emerged
and seedlings circumnutated
breaking ground, and
root brained
warmed in the sun
sprouts swarmed.

The Bending of Summer

So heavy with bees,
the sunflower is on its knees.

                Breathing pores, the birch sheds silver

                                layers, paper bark slivers skein and furl

smoke curls from waxy resin

        weightless traces of drumming places

                                      & feathered leaf tops underwood and

    cord

Breathing pores, the birch sheds silver

layers, paper bark slivers skein and furl

smoke curls from waxy resin

weightless traces of drumming places

& feathered leaf tops underwood and

cord

Poet's tree

Inside February

The tin roof tacks
pinking with the sound of rain
the tin February sky grey
spits on wood pigeons still
sentinel in the ash
the dogs peel bark stripping skin
gnawing branch shards of a storm fallen birch
silver shreddings paper last season's blown tit nests
tinder dry lodged deep in soft moss hollows in split log piles.

February sky tastes of scent of tin
fingers tingle colour of bone flushed cold
the wet dogs breathe warm, and rising damp, we watch the fallow
deer silent tensed lull in their dawn barking to tell
that Spring can't come soon enough.

The dogs trample snow and the sky
drops on aconites piss yellow bruise sour and cyclamen bubble gum
gash purpling pink underpinning witch hazels budding little tails
frothy with lemon ginger bronze and lime.

Under gun metal grey in the scent of rain,
the colours flood water with luminous wash
reflecting back the breast feathers of the brace of wood pigeons,
diving in furious flight,
swimming in the air.

Oak and Owl

a
crisp
dusk

moon

ice
cold

edges

the
owl

slightly
formed

a
tracery

just
there

visceral as cabbage
daffodils

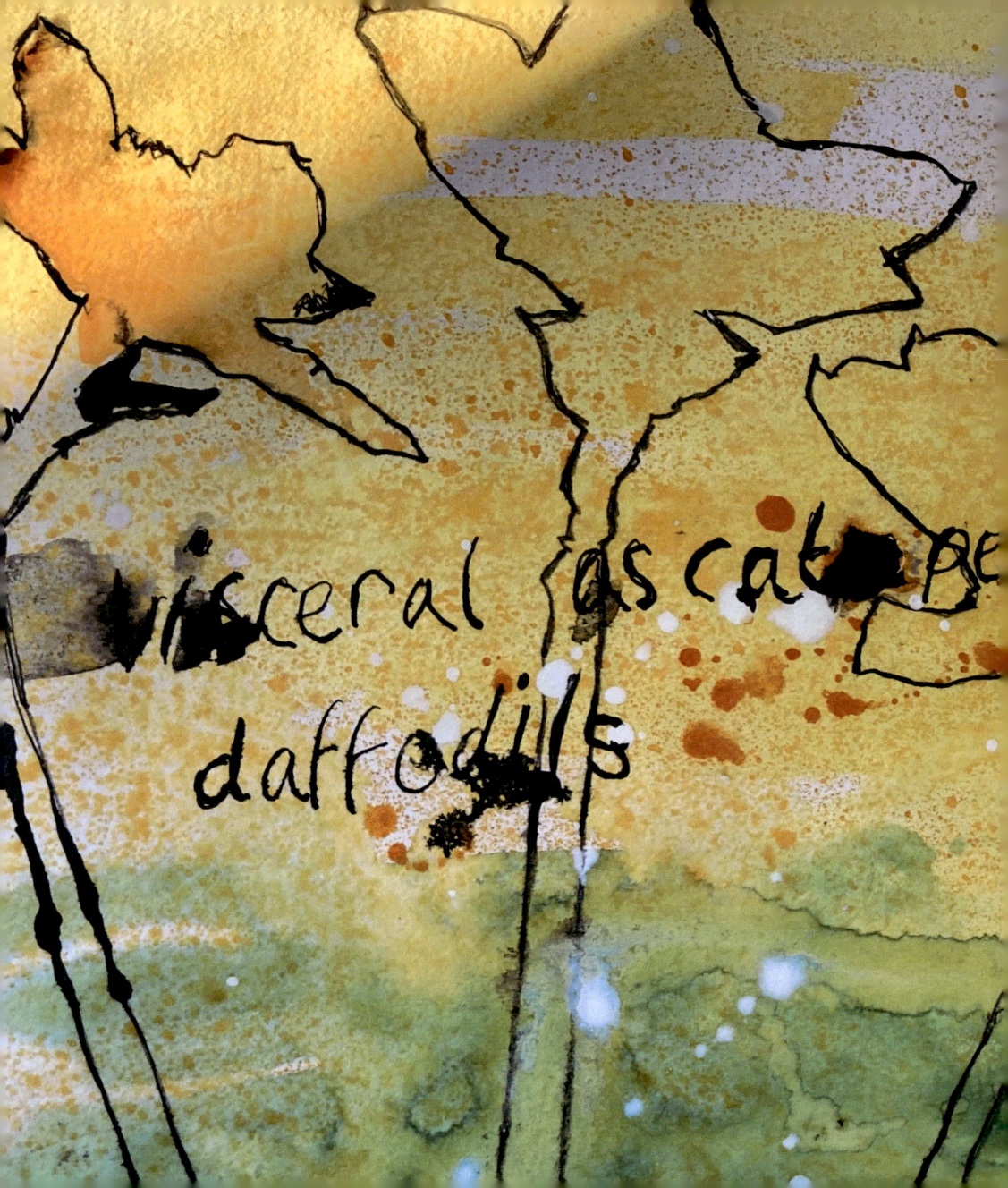

elysian

Obstructing a carriageway

aching
beauty
of
snow
on
bark

The upended birch peels and scrolls fall
brittle text articulates land lore
as snow drops moon-white write
the blind whiteness that is early February sunlight

shards leavening and latticework
lichen spores filter luminosity webbing towering artichoke
mint green wrinkling fringed with lashes
slender branches the colour of bone washes

mist through ledges first creeps to drip black letters
then green fog forms visceral semiotics
then reveals the aching beauty of the birch toss raw
a nuisance in the way of common law.

The upended birch peels and scrolls fall
brittle text articulates land lore
as snow drops moon-white write
the blind whiteness that is early February sunlight

shards leavening and latticework
lichen spores filter luminosity webbing towering artichoke
mint green wrinkling fringed with lashes
slender branches the colour of bone washes

mist through ledges first creeps to drip black letters
then green fog forms visceral semiotics
then reveals the aching beauty of the birch ross raw
a nuisance in the way of common law.

7TH JANUARY

a
few
precise
thorns

articulate

the dog
rose

Gold dust

The dogs and I

sputtered
with
gold

ash

pollen
grains
rain

in field margins
brushing past
seas of stripling grass
rippling oats

spores
emerge
hydrophyte

subprolate
prolate
perprolate

tectum
perforates

spilled,

tree to be,

sun   shadow,

& me

spilled,

tree to be,

sun   shadow,

& me

Belonging

Walking a way

This
morning

the dogs in the
mud and the Spring sun
kicked
over surface
traces and leaves
unhung flung
and the lake sliced by light
spawned

shadow

fenestrating
oaks bough
be neath

by and by
sub marine
silence sliding

we
eyes wide
glide beyond semiotics
to
know

A SHOVEL OF LAND

loam
humus
dried blood
worm casts
bass tea root
dust asp silt
truffled oaks
if fed sea
weed
bud Burst Leaf
old
fossilized
life plea T
t i m e

Ownership of Soil

nd that the soil should
bounded on or towards
eet," and the evidence s
ly a piece of land whic
as held that the soil o

The force of lore articulates Spring rain,
in Clarson, a fence is an offence.

As rain falls, daffodils sour the dull grey sky
the dogs anoint the timber in hot gold
piss and slip beneath the bottom rail, me
climbing
over dank green planks, we walk a way
that's walked every day,
defiance in our defence, and in hope
imagining this land again as a whole,
and watching our breathe as it slows and furls

drifting in spurting crystalline curls,

wet

here where rising light it meets   the sweet

smell of soil

The force of lore articulates Spring rain,
      in *Clarson*, a fence is an offence.

As rain falls, daffodils sour the dull grey sky
      the dogs anoint the timber in hot gold
      piss and slip beneath the bottom rail, me
  climbing
      over dank green planks, we walk a way
      that's walked every day,
      defiance in our defence, and in hope

      imagining this land again as a whole,
      and watching our breathe as it slows and furls

drifting in spurling crystalline curls,

wet

      here where rising light it meets   the sweet

          smell of soil

Between Materiality and Semiosis, or Suppose a Rose

rose rose seed planting seed dormancy
post-harvest seed direct seeding is generally not
germinate before planting generally after
                              stratification
operation methods are as follows cultivation
techniques: roses high high, high sun, cold
and drought
in the northern winter do not need to protect
against frost as long as no drought no watering
can
grow (referring to the ground). The soil is not
strict generally more fertile soil can be loam
muddled mudder
be properly puddled
manure remember and dig spit one spit two
to make strong growth lush blush flush bush
foliage grow well well roses are generally from the
seedlings or seedlings began to plant. During
the year in
addition to
summer
high temperature
is not appropriate the rest
of the season green
watering can
be set or change a rose
sprinkle shower s /pray
water water water
must not be supposed

Choose loose
good ventilation good
drainage of soil cultivation plant
culture
before planting
clay fish bone ash sky fire stone worm
casts
blood after planting
improve the vitality of
watering: root rose can shower and should pay attention to art
/esian basin water dr/ought
to avoid dry
before the flowering to be pelvic
dry before watering
in the watering should avoid pouring from the upper part of flowers
part petals
and trees
water
should be directly poured
into the riparian basin, not to allow the leaves
to wrinkle
a river overnight roots low slow mellow
fertilization: rose fat is very heavy
to tree bees
in addition to planting
flowering period is following every two mouths
for the use of fish fine flow febrile
phloem
to promote
flowering and cellular growing

Sowing then watering the water
before sowing the water, flow
and then the seeds

After slowing, do not be
soil water
seed germination
emergence
stalks flower
if this was it could
bloom do all it toil
soil
should be supposed

    potent

bloom bloom

bloom

In the margins

il crumbled
oamy down
v unpunctured
barks and rolls
purple brown
l plough blades
tween the furrows
g sliding in the
ed the sky

with March

I slipped in the breach and the
and we tumbled into the furro
writ in rows and rows slid down
and the incline dark and the pup
black and the shadows long puc
we scare crows and spit our teeth
shard our ears and straw sheds nest in
gash clay damp cold we plait plas
wet ground, we clawing, up

Apoptosis

Bullocks in buttercups bellow
Bird bones brittle as Spring eggs speckle
A woman in the garden words
Beads of dawn flower sow the lawn
Poppies spit seeds and words are station sown
in groups, three or four at a time, careful to rhyme
Iridescent pink chard stalks
Lemon yellow marigolds
Dithyrambic rain spatters pattern
and troubles the pond surface
Sun swollen bees sneeze and thrum insertions
making incursions into the damp green scene
The word is sticking like pollen to things
and the pigeons flap clatter scatter snapping twigs
Thistles prickle burdock stickles ants' crawl
The wind in the tree waits for rain
and then, the dogs' bark

Garden walls

If I say to you what is a rose and you say to me it is a flower, I may say to you it is the head of my watering can for a shower; or I may say it's the rows of roses in my rose garden or I may say it's the seeds of the cod, cool iridescent wild Atlantic cod roes on toast. Or I may say we may row across the ocean or argue something rotten. Or I may say she's a Rhode Island Red, who laid a perfect blood-warm rose brown egg this morning. That Rose is fatly feathered bronze and glints deep red in the blush flush rose of the dawn sky. She smells of sunlight and dander and makes yolks of liquid gold. A rose is not a rose, is never just any rose. Gertrude would have told Gertrude that. There have to be appropriate rules. Roses have to be read.

And if I say to you that a cell has a membrane and you think it is a skin, I say that skin is misnamed for the membrane of a cell is not a wall nor a shell not a box nor a territorial edge. Is a cell immured, shut up, still, walled in? Is skin a territory? Not at all. Instead, like eye it is the threshold of energetic exchange and may change in space at any moment in time. Interface. Not a one thing still all of the time. Or any of the time. Or at all. Gertrude would have told Gertrude that.

If you [miss] attach a name, a thing becomes some-thing that it is not. And rigid in fact. No what if no what is. Impermeable. Impossible. Immobile. Ceased. The opposite of cells in a leaf. In human. In rose. In a garden. If a garden has walls, it is not a garden. It has ceased.   No garden can be walled. Gardens walk. As we all know. A walled garden has a miss attached name or a wall is not a wall. Gertrude would have known that.

Dead mole in fresh owl pellet

Claws roar in the Ash,
the owls howl down
dawn screaming in the willow
weeping damp limp leaves
low down slow down fall black
bird feathers flutter a loft a drift
de-boned pelleted, velvet and filleted
the sound, a chord cleaved carapace stripped raw.

Growing Things

I suppose we must begin
with the dialectic potential
in the bounding membranes
of chromosomes and spermatozoa.

Matter under
certain conditions
permit the formation
of Nations and colloidal suspensions.

Seeds, on the other hand,
grow where they blow.

Petals

Under the *Stipa gigantea* in early Spring

Kiss close
the toad and eye
both seeing
the butterfly.

Snow Moon (February 2021)

the moon
shucked shelled silvered white bright
as spring garlic skin slipped young
shed brittle in the autumn.

Wild damsons

Cobwebbed tiny sweet rot
damascene
momentous in the hawthorn
shedding tenuous verbal skin,
we slide into now.

Dusk

Words of birds
in the space
between trees.

Dawn

In a white space
a black bird
and the sound
of a crowd of jackdaws.

Composition

Composed
the birch ghosts
white in the morning
mist risen; the earth well versed.

Tines catch a rabbit

Under feet sedge
an edge, ditched
clear over glass and
under sand
flint old and colder
water marks shadows of crows' claw

The oak exhales and the puppy
starts at the sound of a sparrow
hawk shuttering
hollow bones the wind
plays and she soars
and the telegraph wires
strum and the puppy
knits notes of tractor tines and
the harrow turns rows,
and it darts

tiny severed neck bones
little flecks of oxygenated fresh red
shards pale and obsidian deep,
dead as an instant
soft as rabbit fur.

Home grown

As a by-product
of the Lincolnshire wolds and wide low fields
and of the raw coast and tin filled Cornish cliffs
I am
folded
into the land and
into its clefts and in its rows
furrowed
I am
turned
heavy clay lime
lightened adding
texture to land written
down and mined out
hollow as words
and hallowed be.

Wild the why

When making a garden
wild the why is answered by the bees
in D minor and by the newts
flash and by the butterfly

when acres pass in thigh
high grass the why is the why
I am rather than not

feeding failing fledglings, frantic
mother's calling and vixen scream
the sky down and the tawny owl
silhouettes midsummer midnight
and a toad splash

closes water lily petals slant
silver slivers a long grass snake sliding
as pipistrelles dive

the dogs and I make tracks, pollen frass
floats the dogs' coats seed covered
sheen in the white moon
light scattering, they stay close, the owls howl

out the why I make the garden
wild is the why I have no child.

Familial Tree

I do not like me
enough for a different version
of me to stalk into this room, permanently
affixed, growing directly
from my stem.

Or put another way
I do not like me
enough to replicate
and be fractured in the process of
passing on, what?

That of me that I wouldn't
wish on my beloved dogs, my hens,
that which is the best
of the worst of what went before, bad
earth can be fixed, blood cannot

And I know one thing
for sure, that that
shouldn't have been replicated
that fracture continually unearthed is green
sticks in my stem, seeking to grow again.

Sky, hardened

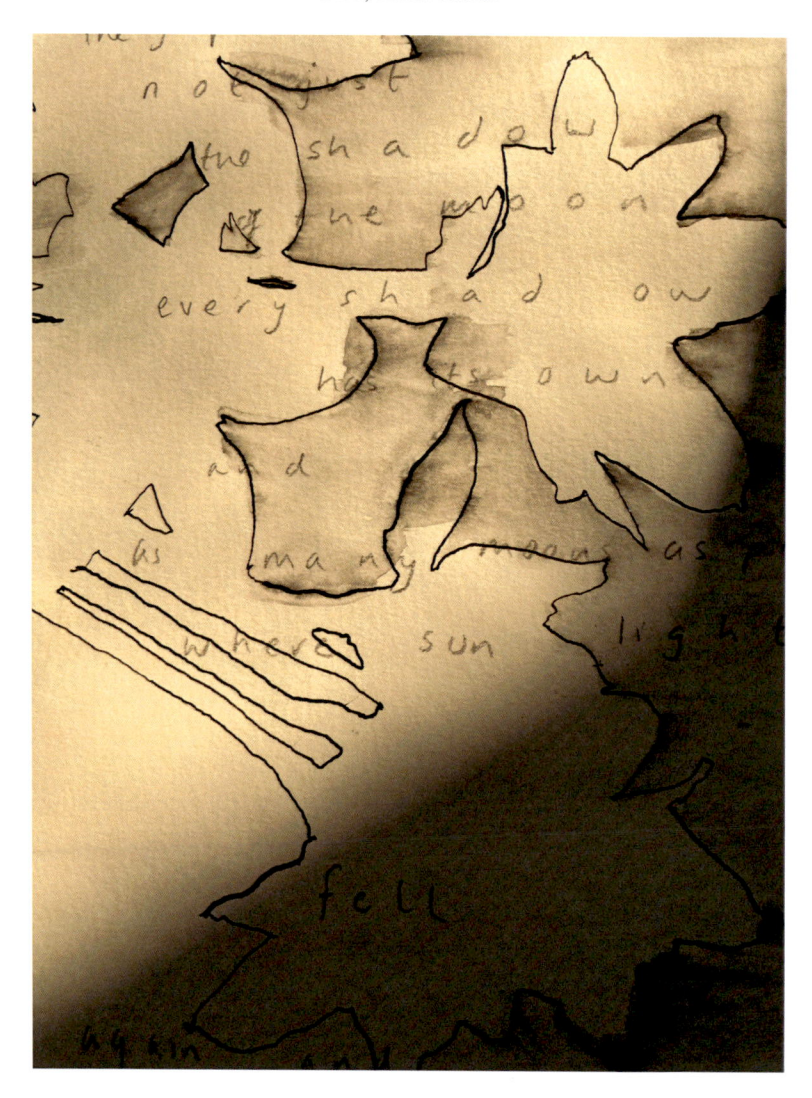

Notes

'Pollarded oak, East Anglian Sanatorium', this oak was pollarded for ship building some four hundred years ago, so was man made multi stemmed. The land beneath and around is riven with its anchors, which both anchor it and make the land in which it is anchored. The given formula in the poem: where tensile strength $(T(r))$ and tensile strain $(\varepsilon(r))$ and modulus of elasticity $(E(r))$ characterise plant anchorage.

'Between materiality and semiosis, or Suppose a rose', inspired by Gertrude Stein.

'Garden walls', also inspired by Gertrude Stein.

'Sky, hardened', in homage to Paul Celan: 'Unwritten things, hardened into language, lay bare a sky', excerpt from 'À La Pointe Acérée', trans. Michael Hamburger.

ink
caps
penetrate
the
paddock
deliquescing
black
inks
spore
filling
soil
pores
gestating
gills
&
caps
once
more

ISBN 978-1-912616-14-5